On Encountering Sorrow

On Encountering Sorrow

Gathu Wahome

Word Branch Publishing

Marble, NC USA
2015

First Edition 2015
Printed in the USA

Cover illustration © 2015 Julian Norwood

Permission can be obtained for re-use of portions of
material by writing to the address below. Some permission
requests can be granted free of charge, others carry a fee.

Word Branch Publishing
PO Box 41
Marble, NC 28905

http://wordbranch.com
info@wordbranchbooks.com

 Library of Congress Control Number: On file

ISBN-13: 978-0692584651
ISBN-10: 069258465X

To all the helpless masses that refuse to rise up and dare to defy or interrogate their sorry political, social and economic conditions.

Acknowledgments:

My deep gratitude to my family, and friends who have provided moral support during the period of writing this book. I'm more particularly grateful to my brother: Nderĩtũ, for his countless acts of kindness and valuable critic. I also salute the Word Branch team for making the publication of this book possible- more so to Catherine Rayburn-Trobaugh.

~~~

The struggle for self-determination has largely gone unsung. This volume is an attempt to recreate human sentiments with vivid imagery. While the content of this book may be specific to a particular geographical region or a person, the themes have a universal outlook. Poetry is a vital force that heals and rejuvenate the mind and heart of its consumer.

Gathu Wahome

Facing the Hill

My old fancy is tens of miles away;
Gut-like- ridges have had us for years stayed.
In the full moon I see her face wax and wane
Facing the hill, my heart begins to pine.
Lingering Scents of her perfume still thrill me with
tremendous intensity
Clutching on her cold pillow, but whom can I blame?
I'd wish to meet her, but I've no means.
Nor writing about nor meeting her in a dream abates my
nostalgia.
In a dim mirror, I see my beard is neglected with care.
I have no desire to groom. Since we parted, I've grown
thin for her.

On Kissing Grief

An itinerant peddler startles me to wakefulness at noon
Suddenly the brew vendor's debts stir in my mind
How much more can I bear grievous toils of this hood?
Surprise, dismay, alarm or pity, deep and profound,
Would show in their looks, with acquaintances of old,
Should we by chance meet again
 In vain, friends of old would sigh, in pain fold,
Their once enviable peer in this deplored state to discover
Do not ask in ridicule, sarcasm with whom I've lost favour,
Instead, alleviate my devastating sorrow with bottle on bottle of scented liquor!

WENDO: In Love

Gĩtanda-inĩ, nduma-inĩ wiki
 Mwĩrĩ ta mwaki
 Agĩthugunda mũhiki

In Love

Spread on bed
Passion boiling red
He's sunk for the nobly bred

26/04/2015: I'm Lonely Still

Heavy traffic snore and rattle
For miles on, chaos and congestion intensify.
An old beggar limps on clutching at a bottle
The homeless gather together in groups, so cold the
crippled one sigh.
I'd love to take her out for tea, but I'm broke
Feeling desperate, I climb up the same joint as usual
Familiar faces all around but I'm lonely still.
The nightfall descends, town-bats awake.
The street flood with lamp lights; my heart fills with
sadness.
What do I think as I listen to my boastful companions?
I feel miserable, bitter about my poor state.

Uprise

Thick mist and dense fog is raw, the earth is cold to the core

In the twilight, and as if in sorrow, a thousand trees hang down their heads.

Real criminals are those opposed to anti-imperialism war,

From Caribbean to Pacific, exiled spirits are still mourning for the dead.

There are many consistent heroes and heroines struggling since days of past

Freedom from state terror is a must!

Those who lead the country without the mandate of the people are our foes,

Let the proletariat up- rise, plus hidden daggers and blazing guns draw bizarre bows

The petty bourgeoisie to annihilate row by row!

15-06- 2015: Pining Away

In the hearth smoldering embers are dying away
Spreading sheets, I sigh to feel my thin quilt steel -cold
The night is lonely, crickets are dreary chirping at the
doorway
Month after month I'll think of you till advanced with
age.

NDIKAUMBŨRA MWOROTO: Strong as Steel

Cirenda ndĩũte mwĩhoko, thũũ kĩrĩgĩrĩro njage
Irenda njoe naigũrũ moko, kĩhoto kũrũĩrĩra ndige
Ndikaumbũra mwototo,kĩama gũkunyanĩra.

mwang'eire mumo, gĩtũmi gũthahia muma
Kĩmĩigue-i mĩraramo, mbĩrĩra-inĩ kĩrĩro gĩkiuma!
Ndikaumbũra mwototo,kĩama gũkunyanĩra.

Ngũaria cararũkũ, amu ndĩ ka-ndeto kanya
Rũthekagĩrĩra rwĩ riko rũkũ; irimũ ningĩ nĩ nyingĩ
mũhuro wa Kenya!
Ndikaumbũra mworoto, kĩama gũkunyanĩra.

Cirenda ngue ngoro, nde mwĩhoko rũtanatema ruoro
Cimemagia na tuororo; mahaki ndarega ngacambio
Ndikaumbũra mwototo, kĩama gũkunyanĩra.

Ndikaũtahĩka, kaĩ kũrĩ wairegi ũtũire?
Nĩrĩkiriĩ Maina na rĩa Mwangi ituĩka; njama na
matharaita nĩĩaũre
Ndikaumbũra mwototo,kĩama gũkunyanĩra.

Strong as Steel

The foe presses hard
So hard that a waverer may yield
But alas! Our will is strong as steel

The dead lay waste somewhere in the backyard
Old and new spirits cry and sigh in the barren field
But alas! Our will is strong as steel

I'd love of the profound to freely speak
But the folly in this land would make each heart break
But alas! Our will is strong as steel

But I'm torn and battered
Torment so severe, how cannot I feel betrayed?
But alas! Our will is strong as steel

It's better to die like heroes of old than live on knees
Look, look, our young men with tools of war are gath-
ered like a forest of trees
Alas! Our will is strong as steel.

28-06-2015: The Calendar Cycle

Heavy mist is all over, the sun is veiled in thick clouds
Tree tips are hanging down, the horizon is dull
The overnight drink has not dissolved effects of my
waist-felt sorrow
Lingering on my pillow, hangover thrills me with dismay
I'd love to brave the dawn but I'm heart broken
Since the calendar cycle ushered in my endless grief
All young blooms have since yellowed

General Kariba (Sep 1954)

Jagged mountain crests soar a million miles in to the foggy air,

At the base, endless mist-shrouded rivers flow rapidly in pairs

Where are the golden monuments of gallant heroes of bygone years?

In these central highlands, General Kariba's name still endure

At the prime of his martial success, the commander had no peer

His great deed at Mũiga still echo from year to year

Of all heroes, I envy best Kariba's countless victories

Preserved both in poetry and patriotic songs are the General's countless exploits.

Should General Waiyaki wa Hinga's spirit

Revisit this our golden land, with May- moon gaily lit,

Avenged, and dancing to a folk song, in shedding rain

He'd this way sigh and say: 'My brutal fate at Kibwezi, after all, was not in vain!'

Kicks Traded with Wild Blows

Knot in a regretful quarrel
Awkward embarrassment follow
Kicks traded with wild blows

The Battle of Chetambe - 1908

Warriors were moistly brave
For the sake of the state, martyrs laid down their lives.
 The battle of Chetambe is legendary;
The heavier the casualty, the gallant the history.

Hands in Sleeves

Petals and colored leaves
  Leaning on the marble eaves
  She admires hands in sleeves

Arap Terer (late 1800- early 1900)

At the prime of his judicial influence:
Kapkiam, Kabuloin and Pinyin kowtowed at his probing glance.
A possessor of peerless talent, a pit of wits,
In his career, Justice Terer pacified all sorts of gruesome crimes and rifts.
Attending trials on the left, those fearful of law, abstained from vice
Litigants from ridge to ridge marveled at his celestial excellence.
At old age, in three occasions, Terer tendered resignation,
But in two plus one occasions indignant sovereigns warned retribution;
It's to a seasoned apprentice wished he transferred judicial authority.
A patriot of unequaled ability,
Even today, his legendary character towers all in integrity.

Intoxicated by Vulgar Pursuits

Intoxicated by vulgar pursuits
 In my youth, I squandered all golden chances chasing after idle passions.
 I still remember prolonged leisure hours in the brothel's inner chambers,
 Made sweeter by liquor and vulgar gift girls
 My bitter regrets now are not few,
 If retrievable, I'd have recalled all the wasted years anew!

Painted Eyebrows

As if in deep, deep contemplation,
 She stares at the endless horizon.
 Steep, steep concerns in her weary face,
 Absentmindedly, she walks by in a lazy pace.

 Her Painted eyebrows are now tilted to the sky,
 Three times she pauses to sigh.
 To fathom, who'd for whom she sheds dim tears
 In the sun set, I see her wander off to the barren frontier.

War for Independence (Oct -1952)

Chain on chain of boundless ranges
Undulate unwillingly to lick dark depths of heavens-
awing gorges
Flanked by deep mist, furious rivers flow east- way
without stop
Enveloped in dew, why do bamboos leaves seem to
weep in drops?

Once and united as one, in these double mountain
boarders
God-like warriors waged war against murderer's in-
vaders
Bound by platoon oath, and commanded by seasoned
leaders,
In droves, a million patriots up- rose in arms for a
legitimate cause
Of these gallant accounts, consult books of poetry and
prose!

Still dotted with ravages of bygcne wars:
Clusters on clusters of death camps dented with bomb
scars!

In these central highlands, millions of peasants and
workers, then
And to dethrone the colonial regime, revolted as one;
Field Marshal Kĩmathi at our armies head forged a War
Council of two plus ten
Victory upon victory is then what proceeded each
wrathful martial mission
Even today the old and the young still talk of the leg-
endary revolution

My Heart is Empty: 27th May 2015

I watch the last blossom fall, before my eyes leaves shed
A whole month has swiftly passed unnoticed
The cold house sits amidst weeds and unkempt grass
Past the dilapidated gate, the narrow path is ridden with
moss
Bare boughs hang down from thick stems small twigs are
tilted in distress
From the ground odd fragrances rise to fuse with chilled
air
My heart is empty, sick with tears
My sad Longing will last for years

Unanswered Texts

Slow, slow is the hour
The night drags on without end
The moon is exactly on top of the glassy tower
Broadcasting her shimmer over the old age land
Glamorous are the side-walk flowers
Yet my pent up sorrow is unbound
My texts mostly go unanswered
Her indifference embitters me profoundly
I'm subdued by the thought of being rejected
Beautiful scenes all around, yet feel so lonely
My agony can only with deep sea be compared

Tom Mboya - 1969

Love of our country led to his early death
 A martyr, time itself cannot waste his heroic deeds
 His illustrious career would away take your breath
 To our regret, Tom Mboya's ambitions were not ful-
filled

April 2012: On Meeting a Rare Beauty

Row on row of seats stretch into infinite columns
In multiple colors, flood lights kindle the spacious hall
The atmosphere is both exciting and calm
But who's the rare beauty leaning against the painted wall?
In a small secluded corner, where lamps are poorly lit
With an acquaintance of 22 or 23, we chat away the gallant minute
Our desires are mutual, we flirt and test wits
A youth so cultured, talented and fine
At her first blush, how cannot I be tempted to disarm with cunning lines?

February 2013: Thoughts on 'Desire'

At this moment I am contemplating the bizarre rural scenery
Hands in sleeves I am facing east- way mutely
About, the colored moon is waxing more brilliantly by the hour
At the horizon, a forest of stars is about to flower

Beginning to reflect on our intimate conversations of times gone by
Gradually, I start to see the futility of pursuing your person
These days I constantly long for your gentle company
And at most vulnerable, how can I refrain from chewing a cud of distress?

Tranquility of the county side is fulfilling but a bit lonesome
On a cold night like this, how cannot I sigh from thrilling nostalgia?
Will re-reading old perfumed letters, exchanged in heat of our younger hours

Gathu Wahome

Startle me from these absorbing concerns?
Oh, how I yearn for our upcoming meeting

Chief Nderi (October 1952)

A perverse traitor of benevolent sovereigns
A lustful -fool corrupted easily with vulgar gains
For favours, rank and prestige, even his motherland he sold
The anti- nationalist stooge, for a dismal title of: Chief, Nderi of Nyeri
 To petty thieves, like Mũrang'a's Senior Chief Njiri
 Mortgaged a noble nation for vanity and fame
A stray dog, ignorant of honour and filial piety
A Homeguard with filth and vomit on his name
By collaborating with terrorists, the Homeguard to his name attracted calamity
At Gura River, swift machetes were what worked the brute's trunk asunder
Our Revolutionary forces tower high for uprooting this awkward elder
A laughing stock for all ages
The villain's death, even today, provokes shame and bitter grudges

I've Come Home Anew

Rows of corn and potato stalks extend beyond sight
 Amidst kales, a forest of spinach is deep green
 The hour is both broad and bright
 Among Peasant sense of hard work is keen
 Raised paths and narrow tracks interlink myriads of villages
 Rows of uniformed ciders, for border, makes the best hedge
 From afar, thick billows can be seen to rise from a thousand homesteads
Near, robust laughter can be heard; it's the dusk mead
At leisure, farmers like drinking up till late
Comparing and contrasting of herds mostly offer the best debates
The sky scraping ridge and the turbid river are at their deepest at the bridge
Look, look gabions are weary with age
Past the lofty hill, a small town should come to view
Oh! I'm come home anew

In Brothel

Gift-girls and liquor
 Extreme Pleasures increase by the hour
 In brothel, intense are the vulgar desires

To Rukia - 2013

Her corpse lay far away and out of sight,
In a narrow grave, who may understand her heart-felt
plight?
Chilled mist and roaring winds all day drive
 At dusk, myriad branches rattle with sorrow
 Pressed by grief, a million owls on funeral stone heave
With melancholy my heart churn and burn; wet is my
thin pillow.

Last year we soared to old tunes
In the leisure hall, hands on hips we indulged in obscene
routines,
 In body and mind our hearts moved as one
 Who'd have thought our brief acquaintance be the last!

My young fancy lay waste a thousand miles from here,
 Revived even if she be, could I take her for a wife?
 After a furious rain, clouds clear,
 My agony persists still; could the parted know my pent-
up grief?

RĨRĨA IHINDA RĨA KINYIRE:
BIDDING FAREWELL

Rĩrĩa ihinda rĩa kinyire
Rĩa kuganĩra ũhoro rĩakinyire
Kuganĩra ũhoro rĩa kinyire
Norĩo thiriti itũ nawe yathirire
Thiriti itũ yathirire.

Rĩrĩa ihinda rĩa kinyire,
Rĩa kuganĩra ũhoro rĩa kinyire
Witũ wendo nawe norĩo wathirire,
Mĩrĩ na ngoro citũ cia thũranire
Mĩrĩ na ngoro citũ cia thũranire.

Bidding Farewell

And then came the hour of parting
our bidding farewell was intense with feelings
And the long separation brew bitter resentment
my regrets so deep, what can I say but lament

Gernal Kalasinga (Sep 5-1954): BATTLE OF KĩGANJO

Turbid rivers sob in streams
In rows, misty waters flow where gorges are dim
What is this place where foggy dews, on broken skulls, teem?
From bombs and grenades, the frontier town
Still lie in ruin since the legendary revolution
I still remember General Kalasinga's posture while adorned in battle gown
So handsome with dreadlocks tumbling down at his every motion
With gun in hand and a swords loftily spread,
How marvelously perfect put he the foe's devices to shame
In years gone by, Kalasinga, and at our army's head
Won early admiration among his peers war of liberation when was at its bitter prime
Few nationalists can match up to the commander's immortal fame
A role model for all ages, years on, patriots still draw inspiration from his awed name

April 2012: On the 23rd Day of Parting

Under a light net
 The back is in a suitable posture set
Feet out spread, I force my person to read,
 It's hard to apply concentration; there is a burning
melancholy in my head

 This is only our first month apart
 Our extreme pleasures of bygone years have now turned
to miserable longing.
 At this moment, what preoccupies your lonely heart?
 Hands lowered at my side, who'd discern my brutal
grieving!

Strange fragrances and odors of old dust are suspending
in my room
Tonight, what sort of mosquitoes are these that hang
from my painted roof?
For how long will I count on fingers the years of separation?
I want axes against those mountains keeping us apart
applied to action

Gathu Wahome

Longing endlessly for you have since topped the list of my idle pursuits,
Can vainly embracing your portrait, on my sick bed, bear fruits?
Tonight, Instead of reciting my pent-up sentiments, as usual, backwards,
Or have my frustration composed on a colored pad
I'll have conveyed my knotty sorrow in a song facing homewards

Abushiri (14th December 1889)

Disgusted by the treacherous acts of the Sultan of Zanzibar
Abushiri dared to defy emperor's orders sent from a far.
A tactician so brave, a martyr with a keen sense of justice
For the sake of our country, the commander se_flessly paid the price
It's the Invasion of our country that forced our General to up rise
Brutality of the foe, our warriors by the horns the bull to seize
At our army's head, the General's martial skills were unmatched
In the battle field, like a kite on wing, his maneuvers were unequaled.

The battles of Tanga and Pangani were grave
But the host successfully overwhelmed the mighty foe
The battles of Kilwa, Linda, and Makindani, proved decisive
For our General's schemes saw German's garriscns fall in rows

Gathu Wahome

But in the battles of Bagamoyo and Dare salaam
(Mzizima) victory was hard to achieve
For well-defended, the garrisons proved impervious to
our army's bullets, arrows

'Captain'Wiszman was a formidable foe
But he could not withstand Abashiri's twanging bows.
The invading forces were keen to capture the reign;
But Abushiri's martial plans were those designed to
frustrate these sinister scheme
Tanzanian nationalism stood profoundly to gain
The German East African Company star if our heroes
caused to wane!

14-05-2014: Come Over My Mind

Thoughts of you have come over my mind tonight
 Next to the study table, am exhausted from longing
 Without, dew pools are radiant with moon bright,
 Leaning against the window I sigh, sigh so hard to hear
your favorite song
 When we parted, we had just been together for two years
Now wild creepers have come to season again, you have
not returned yet
 I'm emaciated, from distress weary. Who will bear my
heart-felt tears?
 The grief of separation is still raw, I cannot bear the
sight of another sunset

02-07-2015: Too Drunk to Stand

An old bird chirps among young boughs
So long that its tears dash down like torrential rain
A dim moon is hanging from a mount capped with snow
Her faded light is broadcasted over the ragged terrain.
There is heavy pressure in my chest
Noises of snapping leaves reminds me of home.
Behind my drink is a pile of sorrow tied to night mist
Too drunk to stand, I sigh to see dawn is come!

General Ndua - (August 1898)

Brave as he was, he could not crush from- the -West- foe
A shrewd schemer although, he could not outwit his fate
General Ndua died in a stormy battle many years ago
While young, he had the talent of serving the state

04-07-2015: Recent Despairs

We seldom texts exchange
Fewer calls still do we make
The first flowers of the season are now advanced with age
Yet from our steep, steep sorrow I do not awake
My temple is wrinkled, my hair thin from pressing cares
Try as I may, thoughts of you still assail me with despair
When I'd thought together we'd always get
Who'd have guessed a life time full of regrets?

Battles for Kabianga (1755-1810)

 Kipsigis's thundering arrows were a constant source of
pain
 To the Gusii, The Isiria Maasai's jagged spears a
horrible menace
 Sandwiched between two mighty foes, how well did
Bantus defend the Kano Plains?
 Did those from Misiri fall in to disgrace?
 The Nyando River belt was a constant source of dispute;
all laid claim to the vast territory
 But the Maasai and Kipsigis, at all cost, were bent on
securing the estates' monopoly
 And thus two plus one nations fell into a protracted
bitter rivalry
Spears and bizarre blades set high to capture victory
And then the Maasia and the Kipsigis tested hands
Slashing and hacking murderously each other's martial
band
And then the Kipsigis's army fell into disarray
Section after section when fell that fateful day
Now the Gusii had to contend with even a mightier foe
To have the Maasai for a bully was pure woe.
Kabianga is a bad place; Kericho is a very bad place

Where our people fell in to a ferocious carnage

The Maasai do not sleep, the Abagusii do not sleep when they remember the battle of Kericho

The Abagusii do not sleep, the Maasai do not sleep when they remember the battle of Migori.

Mama let me go, I go, to the place where General Ole Kericho died

Let me go, I go, mama, let me go to the place where General Nyang'araro died.

Kericho is a bad place, a bad place mama

Kabianga is a bad place, a bad place where our heroes were massacred

Let me go, I go mama to the battle fields where our heroes were massacred

Weathered Leaves

Light and soaring
Reddish cloud is floating
Of dust stirred by fallen leaves.

ŨGŨKIUGA ATĨA?: Which Way?

Nĩkiugo kĩa maa, wangoro ndũrĩ guoya
 Ndũgĩtige gũtheka; one ũrĩa njitire njoya.
 Amu ti kũgũrũka, kũna nĩwendo gũkũnya;
 'kĩo ngũinaina, nĩkĩo ngũtondoira.

Kahinda hee ndĩarie,gũkũnja tiga mĩgũtha
 Reke mwarĩ ngumbũrĩre,wendo ngwĩre ti-macatha
 Ngũthaithe ũndekere, wendo kũremwo 'kũhitha
 'kanjonore kana ũndĩrie, ũgũkiuga atĩa ?

Which Way?

deep, deep are my feelings
For you, my heart's in disarray
ways of romance but grief and humiliation do bring
to desire to possess is like resolving to chase
the wind all my days

On Parting

Dusk clouds drift away
 In tears we part ways
 For years we'll regret this loathed day!

15-05-2014: Seeing Off a Friend

Understanding friends are hard to find
 Seeing you off, I hold back shedding tears
 It's the day we loathed to come

Land and Freedom Army (20th October 1952)

Treachery of the filthy foe discovered,
 Blooming warriors in platoon oath conspired
 Machetes, grenades and bomb in hands
 Three nations contended for stolen lands
 Gĩkũyũ at the van, the Embu assisting the Amerũ martial bands
 Land and Freedom Army engaged barbarians with gallant plans
 General Simba commanded the rear
 General Ndaya flanked with kindled Bren guns at the frontier
 But it's Field Marshal Kĩmathi's shrewd schemes that shook Britons with fear
 Unrivaled in courage and glory
 Our heroes' prestige, from century to century, shall transcend history

Understanding Bedmate

A young lady impedes my homeward way
She insists on supporting me in my drunken stupor
Over a tiny junction, the night is descending swiftly
A restless cricket can be heard chirp among trees
My heart is still wrapped in misery
But her charm is acutely keen, how cannot I feel rather
disarmed?
My pate is dizzy and my deportment light from liquor
I'm rather ashamed to be discovered in this sorry state
Tonight, what sort of hour is this that I find an under-
standing bedmate?

Battles of Merili (late 1790)

With a forest of thick broad- bladed -spears
 Hot blooded Tugen militias raided the Marakwet and routed the Keiyo to the west
 Executing clever military strategies, in pairs,
 Tugen's ranks and files continually devastated the Jemps (Chumus) to the East
 But In the famed battle of Merili, it's said, the Maasai's twanging bows
 Through Tugen's treacherous scheme caused countless holes
 While In the battle of Kebenop-Korongoro caves the Aror Tugen warriors
 In the Pokot's army encountered unexpected terror
 Now routed from the North and cut down in the South
 In their neighbors the Tugens discovered unmatched wrath;
 One day, and beyond the clouds, we'll reunite with all these gallant youths

Past Midnight

Prolonged dog's howling
 Past midnight, few folks are awake.
 It's impossible to sleep; I can't bear the longing
 Try as I may, our heart to heart cord is hard to break.

Highland

In strange array and colors
 Riotous bushes and flowers
 Impeding ridge-side Rivers

Desperate Longing

The dusk sun roves about as if lost
Silver clouds shift and drift without rest
Turning to the dimming east, my heart's still in dismay
It's painful to recount shared pleasure of bygone days
At this moment I'm depressed by our recent fall out
Where you are at, are you engrossed in similar thoughts?

The Battle of Mwala (November 1895)

A traitor, he's deplored from year to year
Deeds of Mwatu Wa Ngoma still attracts disgrace to his name
Mwana Wa Muka's patriotism in contrast has no peer,
His bravery in the battle of Mwala still attracts honor to his fame.

Bitter Winds

Bitter winds blow, clouds drift towards the horizon
Reeds shuffle; the cold river murmur on as it flows
 The hillside is empty; guavas are out of season
 I wander alone, I have no companion
In the secluded path old leaves are yellowing
Year after year I think of you as I watch birds take wing.
 At twilight I return to my bed
I feel so lonely tears dash from my head

Bildad Kaggia

62 years ago, a revolutionary force awoke myriads of assaulted spirits

Bildad Kaggia dared to defy colonial agents in power high

All voices mute, a lone whisper cared to stir with unequaled wits

Now a typhoon of violence swept the world under new heroes when arose to vie

When young he knew how to serve the state,

Long dead although, we still sing sweet tunes for his sake

A Thousand Smokes

Smoke from a thousand homesteads rise to meet the infinite sky
In the grass land, spirits of the dead are lamenting
The winds are gentle, the earth is adorned in a reddish dye
In the recess of the forest, a lonesome raven can be heard grieving
But where are heroes of bygone years buried?
All have passed except for the swift river flowing east to unite with the deep, deep ocean
Past the green hills is the expansive gorge dotted with yellows and reds,
To see old battle fields would break each heart with sad, sad emotions

ŨGŨGĨTWA ATĨA CIRA HIHI?:
Chancing

Ta kĩroo wĩ riri
Ya wendo ndingĩconoka gũkumbũra thiri
ũgũgĩtua atĩa cira hihi?
Nĩtũhĩtũkanĩte maingĩ
Ciĩga igatuĩkanga ningĩ
Ndehũgũra macemania rĩngĩ
Kana guoya kana thoni ndũrĩ
Wendo, wendo nĩ hitho ya erĩ
Ndũgĩũke tũiguithanĩrie mwarĩ!
Tiga ngarari, njinũ na gĩcambio
 Marakara, irumi,maheni; ni waki mwitĩo?
Mũrĩo ũtamĩo: wendo, wendo mũhe gĩtĩo!
Ndagũthaitha ti ũrĩuu kana kũgũrũka
Nĩ na-wendo Ngoro mũrata kũraraka
Ndũgĩtuĩke kinya ihĩndĩ wakwa muka!

Chancing

Coming from different directions

Gathu Wahome

We meet again, oh stranger, so tender
A wanderer to a wanderer, may I pass my salutations
I raise my head and look over my shoulder
She is stubborn, a fit mate for a passionate date
To together wed till advanced with age is our fate

Awkward Lines

The cold invades my bed, teeth rattle in my mouth
The rain increase, I hiss and shiver under the covers
There is no charcoal in the hearth
Stirring the ashes deeply, I sigh at the dying embers
The midnight jet fly overhead; in the recess of the gorge,
voices of insects and frogs intensify
I've no companion to toast, behind my cup I break into a
smothered cry
The night drags on and on, so long that I cannot sleep
So lonely, I approach the study table and jot down some
few awkward lines

Old Melancholy

Records exist of great battles that took place in years
gone by

Horrors and cruelty of war is still fresh in minds of those
alive today

For thirteen years our army's flag leaped high

Our heroes dared to overthrow the colonial regime; seven
decades of procrastination were enough delay.

Of one will a million strong up rose to face the gun
powder

Nor torture, nor death could sink our revolutionary spirit
under.

Of all battles fought, the tragic battle of Kayahwe River
makes the saddest reading

To think of Generals' Kago and Ihũũra may prompt one
to pick up arms anew

Sad, sad are the old war songs

To listen to them in local accent may cause each mouth a
cud of sorrow to chew!

Restless Clouds

Thin and chilled the wind blows in the lonely dusk,
At twilight, July is come again with mist, grief and rain.
My thoughts are sad and heart weary with pressing cares
What can I do, what can I do to rid my melancholy?
Those I envy best reside beyond the clouds
One day we'll unite amidst billion sighs and cheers.

12-06-2014: On Second Thought

The overnight rain have dampened leaves and dust
From top to bottom the ridge is increased with green
New fragrances are soaring to refresh the old crest
At the foot of the mountain columns of households can
be seen
All my life, my thoughts have been those of running a
business,
Instead I suffer hardship, lacking money, employment
was never what I wished
My entrepreneurial companions are mostly rich, what
plans have I but to retire to idleness?
To lie on grass and a drunken solitary life is regretful
indeed.

General Mbaruk:Battles of Mombasa (1895-96)

The sky and ocean turned to the color of night
At the horizon a formidable foe when came to sight
A Fleet of mattock- like canoes and warships shadowed the great coral reef
The foe's Cannons and guns, to Mombasa, when pointed from the broad deeps
Now the ones from West and those from Southeast for the first time encountered,
A million barbarians' and murderer's hounds, at dawn, when anchored
War bugles and roaring drums are what set out the tempo for corking riffles
Rival bands when finally locked horns in an earth wrecking battle
Now those from Sudan, Egypt and India were called in to reinforce the savage foe,
Stronger, those from the West now renewed the offence in rows,
Lo! The battle took unexpected turn, General Mbaruk was now in peril

First Day of the Strike

Tanks and rifles over shadow streets
Chaos and contradiction intensify
There are up to it again
Scholars of nowadays are not like of old

July 2008: Hollow Tunes

The deep, deep green grass turn yellow in the chilled
mist
Before the last flower fall, old clouds press high against
the snowy crest
Since times of old cycles have alternated without inter-
ference
This year, why should gorges and valleys roar in griev-
ance?
Great winds are combing through vast Eastern lands
Thousand bamboo tubes are weeping and issuing with
hollow tunes
The night is cold, so cold that my agony is without end
To listen to the pattering rain breaks my heart in to two

26-04-2014: Countless Coups

Countless coups have left the land in shambles
It said lust for power has sired but grief and death
Since ancient times sons have buried fathers in times of peace
But alas! In times of war fathers have buried ambitious sons
Great rebels make enduring heroes
Great although they perish without trace

July 2006: Season of Pain

From the forest floor fumes rise, in the dusk wind thick
mist sway
The hour is old, guns silence momentarily
Beyond this ridge is the Death Valley
In its belly are piles on piles of a thousand years decay
We swore on oath you and I
Wail or groan, meet or part, live or die
We capture the capital tonight

2010: A Small Boat

A small boat hacks furiously through the liquid road
At the vessel's head waves on waves divide in to two.
I left this land when unmarried, I now return with a grey
head
Exiled for so long, who'd know my bitter rue?
I fear friends of old may not recognize my weary locks
To learn but a handful are still alive insights endless
brooks

Battle for the Frontiers-Early 1800s

Vast territories turned to treacherous battle grounds
Nilotes and Bantus, for prestige, when tested hands.
The Clamor for commerce and monopoly of estates was
the constant source of rifts
Followed by Covetous nature of the guest towards the
host's profits
Though constant suspicion and aggression of the Maasai
towards the Agĩkũyũ
Is what initially kindled cold resentment
Which broke the camel's back was the nomad's extrava-
gant arrogance.
For the sake of peace pact, at one point,
Highlanders had tolerated dwellers- of- the- plains
extravagant arrogance
In order for hostility to cease, at one point,
Dwellers of the plains had temporarily abound by the
solemn covenant
But alas! The peace treaty defiled,
How could war tools not be employed?
Now two state fell in to protracted war
To draw broad spears and bizarre machetes implied
causing opponents with fatal scars!

Tied in Knots

Around the pool they cluster in threes:
Thick pine trees
Leaves and creepers are tied in knots
Among boughs is a colony of liverworts
An array of flowers line my homeward way
Stepping on a ragged stone I linger to admire the scene
I often do in this place delay
Season after season rare beauties, knitting, are often seen

ŪTHAYA RAID (5- 8-1953)

At the head of a god-like army
The General, to Ũthaya, set out for a revolutionary
mission
Confident and extremely cautious,
His ambitions were not petty to the politically conscious
In his mind, profound strategies took form
Mathenge's calculated plots were without error
His martial schemes were those tailored to bring about
radical reforms.
At the frontline, buzzing bugles are what first fed the foe
with utter horror
But it's the thunderous roars of flowering guns that threw
barbarians in to quagmire,
In to panic and pain, unexpected waves of murmuring
fire
Our General's task complete,
The Black Jack to the ground brought, the enemy suf-
fered defeat

14-05-2014: Murmuring Dew

Without dew is murmuring
Within the tap is weeping endlessly
Tonight, what sort of melancholy does the hour bring?
I regret countless letters dispatched without reply
The noise of traffic and homing drunkards is dismal,
So lonely is the capital.
Why am I so stubborn to absent myself from her for so
long?
 In a dream, she is far off, I call on her in vain.
I rise and sit, but alas! I find no peace; I cannot bear the
longing.
When young, I knew no sorrow, but now I'm steeped in
miserable pain

Battles of Iveti (August 1898)

To our regret, her ambitions were not fulfilled
Loyal although she was, the commander fell in to bitter
disgrace
General Syonguu was in the art of war perfectly skilled
But in the battle of Iveti the partisan army succumb to
the foe's crushing force
To the capture of General Mwana wa Muka, the foe
owed its victory,
To the surrender of General Nzibu Mweu monopoly of
our lady's vast territory
Brave as she was, our heroine could not the day carry!

Cud of Melancholy

First blossoms of the season show
Array of flowers are arranged in rows
The lash grass is like a deep sea on the endless plain
Swallowing up all paths of the Southeast rains
A desolate house stands in the recess of a shaggy bush
In an empty court yard only a few long-beaked fowls
keeps me company
Last year we held hand on this spot, our faces were
laughter washed
This year I sit alone chewing a cud of melancholy.

Thinking of Home

The forest-side town fall desolate at twilight,
Gradually thick shadows sweep down empty streets
Rattling of speeding traffic reach us at the cemetery site
Stoned, we puff and sip some more; we're slightly over
eighteen
It's the thrill of our lives
Losing home way, we blunder and stagger till cock five

The Treaty of Machakos (08 -4 -1898)

To collaboration chiefs owed their crowns
To cruelty their countrymen's loyalty
Masaku and Mbole wa Mathambo were traitorous clowns
Too Eager to stoop at the invader's flattery, what a pity
And the land they had held so long passed from them forever,
With the treaty, liberty and initiative never autonomy to recover

1-1-2015: Young Beauty

A young beauty delays me with whispers and tender play
She pleads with me to keep her company till dawn
In the stray moon light her form is in full display
Before a set bed, I watch her shed a light gown
The night is both deep and slow
Behind an egg-shaped window we toast and drink up
Music and delicious food keep us aglow
Bodies turn; we refill our cups
Curtains up roll; scented candles weep away
Low Winds rustle; old mist dim down the town
Till advanced with age, here, a wanderer by another may
merrily stay
But my home yard is far away from here; before dawn,
off I set.

Banners

Along the street our banners leap
To the gate a thousand strong march on
Peasants dare vie for power high
The worthless at ransom are fond of holding the nation
Hyenas and stray dogs are used to plunder and gruesome
betrayal
The sovereign is intolerably corrupt and disloyal
Who is this sowing the proletariat with poverty and
sorrow?
It's time to insurrect, pick them guns and bend bows
Repugnant rodents and parasites to feed with woe

31/03/2015: In Disarray

Strong winds blow in the rainy season
Dark cloud hang down from the sky
My mind is tangled in endless considerations.
At dusk a report from home come in with a sad reply
In the moonless night, my grief is keen.
The tidings of his being taken ill sorrows me deeply,
He daily query's what date I can be seen
Oh! I'd pay him a visit but I have no means and my
home district is far away
What can I say circumstances so dire?
All I can do is regret the passing days.
The pole-stars turn; chilled dew put out the last signs of
fire.
My heart is in disarray.

5/26/2015: Facing the Gun Powder

Day and night war rages, our sorrows multiplies without
stop
Since the campaign begun many bitter years have vainly
passed
Captives are used to facing the foe's noose and drop
But what loyal solder would the oath have betrayed?
Like torrential rains bombs daily fall on us, our wounds
with blood leak
Air-crafts assaults are severe, but our will is too strong to
break
Tidings from home no longer reach the frontiers
Cut off doleful songs of childhood, from nostalgic
solders, move me to tears
I entered the forest at 18, at 31, I'm still facing the gun
powder,
Have you not seen pile on pile of faded bones at border
towns?
We march over vast territories, dew wet our battle
gowns.
What year will sovereigns old grudges bury and sign a
truce?

That day we'll slaughter a goat and with ours foes dance, embrace.

Fears

Amidst drizzling showers I'm alone
Locks are wet and my feet dirty
This morning the sun brightly shone
But amidst crooked trees and wide valleys the air was
empty
I sighed to think of home
 I often fear I'll die poor and miserable

4/30/2015: Comradeship

A strange bird croon, atop jagged crests a young sun
come to view
The day is bright, driving winds hasten rare plants to full
bloom.
Old barks peel off from crooked trunks torn liverworts
fall; my thought begin to turn to you.
Broke, we rarely met, financed however together we'd
always get.
Seeking pleasure, we often roamed from town to town
Only when broke would we from leisure chambers
depart.
Rain falls at twilight to add weight to my gown;
My old companion is deep, deep in heart.
Between us is a thousand miles of thorns and briars
To think of you thrills my heart with sad, sad tears.
When we bid farewell who'd have guessed it'd be for 15
years!

Revolution Time

Red liquid add color to petals
After a vicious battle grave groans split the air.
Our enemy's headquarter is in the capital
Orders out, we march on in pairs.
The campaign has raged on for twelve months in a row
Our banners flying high we bring down the high wall.
The tyrants hold is on the decline- mighty are our twang-
ing bows
Only when the extravagant regime falls
Can the proletariat power seize

General Mbaka: September 1956

Loyal to the last
General Mbaka's faithfulness is un-paralleled
Captured although, in courage, he tops the list
His martial schemes are legendary, his talent unmatched
Bitter years those endured he countless stubborn battles
I wonder what date we'll unite with the gallant immortal

The Long Rains

Distressed birds twitter and sigh among branches
A bunch of monkeys chatter and jump from tree to tree
Listening to sounds of nature I sit legs out stretched; hard is the bench
Leaves are yellowing, dust is spread all over like an infinite sea
The long rains have either forgotten this place or have lost their way here
The river's current is weaker than last year's!

Old Companion

Rowdy bats fly about
From night dew grass is wet
The horizon is thin and stretched out
Amidst foggy clouds are echoes of a sleepless eaglet
Thick are the fumes from the disc-like pool which rise
Old are the yellow leaves on the ground which scatter
Regrettable are columns of flowers which weather.
The sombre night scene reminds me of my old companion
To contemplate times gone by thrills me with sad emotions
The teary grass is long enough to swallow my feet
 Loitering the compound, oh! How desperate I've grown.
The mountain air is chilled, mid-year scents are sweet
Ridges are silent, valleys are gently flowing down
Our separation has lasted for year
To think of my bosom peer fills me with endless tears

To Nijo

The lamp cast dull shadows on my wall
Embers die down as the charcoal stove grow cold
Minutes after I pick the call
 I learn of his fall, oh! Barely two and a half decades old
And I recall fondly what merry made we in years passed
by
Who'd have guessed our brief encounter be the last?
I cry, with turbulent winds the rain sigh
My heart is veiled in sorrowful mist
Tonight I drink alone without cheer
Nauseated by gin but unable to puke, how cannot I break
in to bitter tears?
And though the endless river flows to the unknown never
to return
Years after year my tears will endlessly run!

The Battle of Mukuyuni- (November 1895)

Commander Mwana wa Muka dared to subdue a formidable foe

A million arrows when ordered shot forth from eager bows

The enemy was gathered like a forest of trees at Mukuyuni military base

All over Iveti region ominous clouds were spread as do wind on water surface

But the aggressor's incursion had disastrous repercussions

A simple stroke of the General's right, and the foe encountered total annihilation

Bitter Grief

Depressed from pressing cares I sit on bed and hum to a tune

Last year was riddled with despair, this year, what misfortunes!

The midnight cold thrills me with pain

Long hours of sleeplessness has worn me with bitter grief

His corpse lay far away in the sighing rain

Gulping cup on cup still brings no relief

At the door step, young flowers are weep away

Try as I may I cannot forget companion of my younger days

Oh! My sorrow will last for years

Reflecting on Rare Beauty

She looks back at me and her eyes are still
She smiles then hurry's towards the hall
Though kind are her words, she often make light of
promises she has made.

Martyrs

It's no wonder flies and mites should shiver in the wind
Around the capital a furious storm is on the rise
Let each gun find place in our heroes hands
The 53 year old loathed reign revolutionaries to bring to
a close
The western lake is bright in the moonlight
The central mountain's equal to heavens in height
Heavy casualties should not our radicals deter
By generation after generation homage is often paid to
martyrs

Last Night Sentiments

Pools are bright, waters are calm, only noises of restless
ripples can be heard
The earth is damp, cold is the night; few are the noctur-
nal birds
On the small bridge is a pair of fresh footprints
The sleepless one is sighing again, so hard that his
sleeves are wet
The hour is misty, heavy is the wanderer's torment
The year has passed without trace, his dear has not
returned yet
I wonder what year she'll reunite with her fine mate

NYũMBA NA RIKA ITIUMAGWO WAKINĨ!: Comradeship

ĩka ũrĩa ũgwĩka, itirĩ marũrũ njĩka na njĩka
Ndiretigĩra yakwa gũitĩka
Thakame yaitirwo nĩ ũndũ wa wĩyathi na ithaka.
Nĩndarega thata ya bũrũri gũtwĩka,
gũkunyanĩra Kenda mũiyũru gũikia icuanĩ.
nyũmba na rika itiumagwo wakinĩ!

Ndagũthaitha na nguo ya nyũkwa
Menya kĩrĩndĩ gũkendia ũkombo-inĩ
thahu gũkagwata, gukaringwo ni ngwa!
nyũmba na rika itiumagwo wakinĩ!

Cianangera ngero thũũ;
 thakame ikanjita kamatimũ
No wakwa mũrera nĩ mũmũ!
Na Kihoto na ũmaa ndigatiga kũrũĩrĩra wakinĩ
nyũmba na rika itiumagwo wakinĩ!

Ciananyarira thũũ getha ndĩ-umbũre,
Ikahũnga mahũri njirũngi ithecete ikere
No nĩngũmĩrĩria mĩnyamaro ngiya ũtukũ ũthere,
Amu Ngai itũ ĩrĩ mbere.

Gathu Wahome

No ngatoria magerio ona mũnyarare!
nyũmba na rika itiumagwo wakinĩ!

Ndĩ werũ-inĩ,arata nĩmandiganĩirie,
Ndĩ hatĩka-inĩ,no nĩnũmĩtie,
Ndĩ irima-inĩ, ndũgĩũke tũteithanie!
nyũmba na rika itiumagwo wakinĩ!

Mwahirĩre ithamĩro, ndanyarirĩka ngue ngoro
ndigũte kĩrĩgĩrĩro kana mwĩhoko, no rũgateme ruoro.
guũria-i arata matharaita, rikai kuo tigai kũmemia haro
gũtirĩ yuraga na ndĩkĩe, kaĩ mũtaraigua gatwa ũhoro?
nyũmba na rika itiumagwo wakinĩ!
nyũmba na rika itiumagwo wakinĩ!

Comradeship

I'm used to stubborn war and bitter fighting
Like heroes of old I often make light of death
Empty threats cannot break my will strong;
To purge foxes holding the nation at ransom will improve both
our wealth and health

And so traitors like dogs will die
For our sake when thunderbolt come from the sky
To purge foxes holding the nation at ransom will improve both
our wealth and health

On Encountering Sorrow

A new hero dare to defy evil omen
Bourgeoisies are but maggots gorged from skulls of men
To purge foxes holding the nation at ransom will restore both
our wealth and health

For what should a martyr grow weary or despair?
A sudden moon is breaking through the night air
To purge foxes holding the nation at ransom will restore both
our wealth and health

We swore on oath you and I
Atrocities so severe may I sigh?
To purge foxes holding the nation at ransom will improve both
our wealth and health

Exiled for so long, I wonder with what men I can conspire
Its time in our country for new heroes' new height to aspire
The wave of revolutionary violence in each heart should burn
as do the wild fire
To purge foxes holding the nation at ransom will restore both
our wealth and health

Draft and Chess

We play draft and chess
By the pool deep green is the grass
We notice not time fly
At the horizon the dusk sun is shy
We play draft and chess
And although idle we enjoy ourselves nonetheless
When cold, few people dare visit the park
Flowers to maturity grow till weathered with age
We play chess and drink, we realize not the night approach,
And although we're unemployed, we enjoy ourselves nonetheless

The Hour We Loathe

You listen so well, so kindly to my pity
Turning in different directions, it's the hour we loathe
Tonight the ridges will separate us
And then, when we have parted awhile, grief anew
And As I always am with your love in my heart
Many irksome dates will pass between us in bitter rue

July Air

The July air is unusually clear
The young moon is bright with white beams
There is plaintive sound of rustling winds in my ear
Gurgling noises can also be heard issuing from far off
streams
My longing at this hour is profound
But not as the floating clouds that seem to have no end

Tired

The night is awfully silent
Under the floating clouds dew drops are without count
Oh, I feel so sad, sad to think of my companion of old
I'd hoped together we'd always get
But alas! Who'd have guessed a lifetime of regrets?
I lie and toss, but no matter how hard I try, I cannot fall
asleep

Late Night

Dogs fight all around, the compound is vibrant with chaos
In recess of my house I've no companion to share idle dialogues
I cry, can't you see my shadow's wet
Ten cups still won't drown my infinite despair

Old Days

The room is crowded, the air is tight
There is a small moon floating in the twilight
I look at the boundless sky and sigh to see the gloomy
horizon
In the mirror, I see sad times pass, oh, I've no companion
Vaguely I seem to understand futility of laying bare my
heart
I regret the countless years spent apart!

General Olekisio(03-09-1954)

New courage filled each hero's heart
With rare passion countless blades descended on the foe
And the firing mortars, thick like grass, were rent apart
Our patriots routed enemy forces in rows
Read down the names through all the years,
Of Generals that masses hold in awe
Than Ole Kisio you will not find among his peers.
General Ole Kisio died a long time ago
His great deeds in the battle of Narok are with us still

Lover's Heartbreak

The first quarter of August moon brightens the sphere
The expansive lands spread out to meet up with the infinite sky
The winding rivers are full and clear
Songs of frogs and crickets rise up to pierce clouds high
At the terminus we're alone, our sleeves are wet
We face each other holding hands, too overcome to speak
Tonight we part in different directions, never again to together get
To think of this may make each heart weak

December 2013: To Land and Freedom Army

Fireworks light up the capital

For a thousand miles colorful lamps can be seen

We pour libation where grass is most green

And drink up to see the flag sour proud with each chant

Drums roar and lyres increase in tempo, the moon come to full display

The crowd is charged, the occasion is elaborate and guests elegant

At sight of black, green and red all feelings of sadness and conflict melt away

Tonight we celebrate heroes of bygone years

To think back six decades moves our patriots to tears

Fateful Day

The fateful day of the colonialist came in the reigns of
Mitchell and Baring

It is true the two were incompetent weaklings, too timid
for their times

The last days of the empire approached and weapons
clashed with violent bangs

In every quarter, this land suffered stress of war and
murderer's crimes

Imperial terror was rife,' Erskin, the fascist, tyrannized
the state

In reserves, peasants wailed, in travail infants wept in
poor state

But those in support of the movement

Nor hope of life nor fear of death could waver our
heroes' oath

Then the Central Committee ordered absolute commit-
ment

And great generals, moved with anger, rallied our gallant
youth

Commander with commander strove and dared to raid
the enemy's lair

Dealing savages with wondrous woe and bitter despair

Gathu Wahome

Operations, Anvil and Mill Town, were futile schemes
tailored to thwart our guerrilla
Sinister Imperial propaganda was the foe's final sole
pillar
Of the warriors of that time matchless Tanganyika was
the boldest
The general's valor and prowess tops our martyrs list.

The Hour

The clock's arm swiftly away sweep the hour
Our dialogue grow more intense and sincere by the
second
We do not notice the sudden shower
So absorbed, the old sun finds us deeply drunk, sadly my
stay has come to an end
It's time to bid farewell, the full moon breaks through
heaven's breast
Seeing me off tears overrun ours chests

About the Author

Gathu Wahome is a writer and lover of poetry and resides in his native Kenya. Gathu has been writing for the past ten years, and is currently polishing up his second volume of poetry, 'Early Misfortunes', following On Encountering Sorrow -- his debut publication.

Gathu Wahome is the brother of the award-winning author, Ndiritu Wahome.

~~~

If you liked *On Encountering Sorrow*, please leave feedback.

You can email Gathu with your questions and comments at gathuwahome@wordbranchbooks.com.

For a limited time, you can get 10% off your entire book order from Word Branch Publishing. Enter the code CD10 at checkout. https://www.wordbranch.com/book-shop.html

We recommend these books:

Sugar Takes Her Coat Off
Can't Fight the Verse
By John Opskar: http://www.wordbranch.com/john-opskar.html

Feel Your Soul
By Ieva Salina: http://www.wordbranch.com/feel-your-soul.html

The Girl with the Flawless Face
By Ndiritu Wahome: http://www.wordbranch.com/the-girl-with-the-flawless-face.html

Word Branch is an independent publishing company located in the heart of Appalachia. We represent talented new and emerging authors who need a venue to make their voices heard. Visit our online book shop and discover a world of imagination, facts, stories, and entertainment. Written by some of the finest rising stars in the book world, Word Branch Publishing offers a diverse selection of drama, science fiction, personal growth, young adult, indigenous titles, and more. https://www.wordbranch.com

Word Branch Publishing:
Independent Publishing
For Independent Readers